My DISNEY

STARS AND HEROES 2

Workbook with eBook

Viv Lambert and Cheryl Pelteret

Welcome

 ✏️ 💬 **Look and write. Then ask and answer.**

1

It's _____ o'clock.

2

_____ twelve _____ .

3

It's _____ _____ .

4

_____ _____ o'clock.

> What time is it?　　It's seven o'clock.

2 ✏️ **Find the numbers in the picture. Circle and write.**

a

24 / **(42)**

forty-two

b

96 / 67

_____

c

31 / 37

_____

d

58 / 85

_____

e

54 / 45

_____

f

93 / 39

_____

I can ask and answer about the time and say numbers 20–100.

1   **Write the days. Then listen and check.**

Saturday Sunday Thursday Tuesday Wednesday

| Monday  | _____  | _____  | _____  |
| Friday  | _____  | _____  | |

2 **Look at 1 and match. Then choose and write.**

I can make
new friends.

dance   Fridays   play soccer   Thursdays

a
On Tuesdays, I _____ .

b
On _____ , I play the guitar.

c
On Saturdays, I _____ .

d
On Mondays, Wednesdays, and
_____ , I swim.

3 **Draw and write for you in 1. Then say.**

On _____ .
I _____ .

 **Choose your favorite
activity in the unit and stick.**

I can name the days of the week and share personal information.

1 We are different

Learning Heroes

Words I know	Words I want to learn
tall short fast	_____
_____	_____
_____	_____

Video quiz

1 ▶ **1A** **Watch again and do the quiz.**

1 ✏ Read and number.

(a)    (b)    (c)    (d)

1 She has a fast horse.

3 He's big and strong.

2 She's a teacher.

4 He has a sister and two brothers.

2 ✏ Circle. How does Mom feel? Why?

(a) **sad / excited**

(b) **bored / angry**

2 🖊 **Choose and write.**

| fast | short | strong | tall |

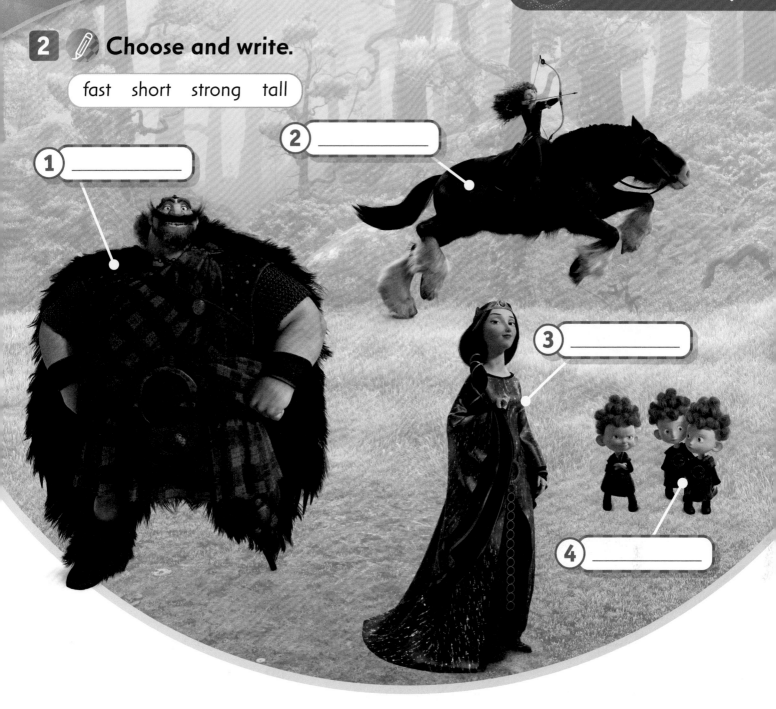

1 _____

2 _____

3 _____

4 _____

3 Challenge! 🖊 **Find and write. Where does Merida live?**

a	l	c	t	s	e
1	2	3	4	5	6

She lives in a ___ ___ ___ ___ ___ ___ .
　　　　　　　　　3　1　5　4　2　6

🕐 **Extra time?**

Close your books. Use the new words in sentences.

 describe people.

5

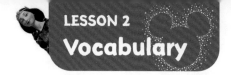
1 🎧 1.1 ✏️ Listen and match.

Ellie   Marco   Charlie   Suzie   Bella   Sam

2 ✏️ Look at 1. Choose, write, and circle.

beard   blond   curly   dark   gray   long   straight

a

Name: _____

Eyes: brown

Hair: short, _____ , dark

Glasses: **yes** / **no**

b

Name: _____

Eyes: green

Hair: _____ , straight, _____

Glasses: **yes** / **no**

c

Name: _____

Eyes: brown

Hair: _____

and a _____

Glasses: **yes** / **no**

d

Name: _____

Eyes: blue

Hair: short, _____ ,

_____

Glasses: **yes** / **no**

⏱ **Extra time?**

Make an identity
card for you. Draw,
write, and say.

 **I can** describe appearance.

1  Read and circle.

1 Is he tall or short?

He's **tall** / **short**.

2 Does he have a beard?

Yes, he does. /
No, he doesn't.

3 Does he have blond hair
or dark hair?

He has **blond** / **dark** hair.

 🧩 Number and write.

 he   short?   ls   or   tall

_____

2 Draw someone in your family. Then circle and answer.

1 Is **he** / **she** tall or short? _____

2 Does **he** / **she** have
a beard? _____

3 Does **he** / **she** have short
hair or long hair? _____

4 Does **he** / **she** have curly
hair or straight hair? _____

⏰ **Extra time?**

Ask or write two
questions about a
friend's picture.

I can ask and answer about appearance.

Different is fun!

1  **Read and match.**

1 Who doesn't have a picture on the wall?

2 Who has blond hair?

3 Who's tall?

4 Who has short, brown hair?

ⓐ Pedro

ⓑ Laura

ⓒ Daisy

ⓓ Amelia

2 ✏️ **Draw you in the story. Write.**

It's OK, Daisy. Only I _____ .

Only I have red hair.

3 💡 **Which picture do you like? Check (✔).**

1

2

⏱️ **Extra time?**

Think about your friends. What's special about them? Write or say.

8

I can read and understand a story.

1 🖊 Look and match. Then write the numbers.

ⓐ
ⓑ
ⓒ
ⓓ
ⓔ
ⓕ

| ride a scooter | ☐ | cook | ☐ | horseback ride | ☐ |
| play the drums | ☐ | take pictures | ☐ | play basketball | ☐ |

2 🖊 Choose and write.   basketball cook horseback play ride take

❶ I can _____ the drums. I can't play
_____ or _____ a scooter.

❷ I can _____ ride and I can
_____ pictures. I can't _____ .

3 🖊 Choose and write.   ~~cook~~   horseback ride   play the drums
ride a scooter   take pictures

inside
both
outside

cook

_____
_____
_____

_____
_____
_____

🏠 **English at home**
Sing the song for your family!

(**I can**) name free-time activities.

1  **Listen and number.**

a

b

c

✿ **Number and write.**

 can

 jump.

 Angus

_____

2 🖊 **Complete and check (✔) column 1 for your family member.**

	① My _____	② My friend's _____
run fast		
draw		
ride a scooter		
cook		

3 💬 🖊 **Ask a friend. Complete and check (✔) column 2.**

Can your sister run fast?

No, she can't.

⏰ **Extra time?**

Write or talk about your family member. He/She can . . .

10

I can  ask and say what people can do.

Understanding others' feelings

1 🖊️ 💡 **Choose and write. How do you think they feel?**

| angry   excited   happy   sad   worried |

1 She's _____ .   **2** He's _____ .   **3** They're _____ .

4 He's _____ .   **5** She's _____ .

Oh, no! My T-shirt!

This is fun.

My friend isn't here.

Oops! I'm sorry!

Thank you.

2 💬 🖊️ **Ask a friend how they feel and why. Draw and write.**

My portfolio

I'm sad. I don't have a bike.

It's OK. I don't have a bike.
We can walk!

⭐ **Be a hero!** ⭐

Mime a feeling.
Can your friend
guess?

I can say how someone feels.

Drawing faces

1 🖊 **Look and number in order. What's missing? Draw.**

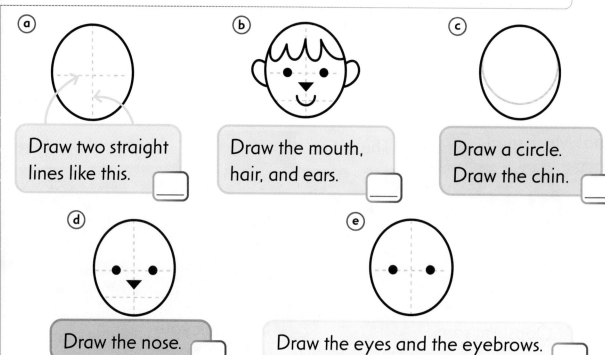

ⓐ Draw two straight lines like this. ___

ⓑ Draw the mouth, hair, and ears. ___

ⓒ Draw a circle. Draw the chin. ___

ⓓ Draw the nose. ___

ⓔ Draw the eyes and the eyebrows. ___

2 🖊 **Look. Then write the capital letters and periods (.).**

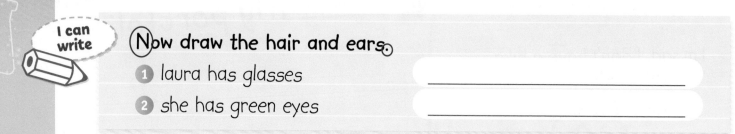

I can write

(N)ow draw the hair and ears(.)

❶ laura has glasses _____

❷ she has green eyes _____

3 🖊 **Draw a face and hair. Look at 2 and write.**

_____ has _____

_____ has _____

I can understand, draw, and write about a face.

⏱ **Extra time?**

Show and tell your friend about your picture.

My friend poster

1 What do you know about your friend? Put a ✔, ✗, or ?. Then ask questions to find out more.

My friend is ...	My friend has ...	My friend can ...
tall ◯	straight hair ◯	ride a scooter ◯
fast ◯	long hair ◯	run fast ◯
strong ◯	brown eyes ◯	horseback ride ◯
_____ ◯	glasses ◯	play the drums ◯
	_____ ◯	_____ ◯

Ask your friend questions.

Are you …?

Do you have …?

Can you …?

2 **Create** Think and complete for your poster. Then write and draw.

⭐ **My friend** ⭐

My friend's name: _____

He / She is _____.

He / She is _____.

He / She has _____.

He / She has _____.

He / She can _____.

My friend has curly hair.

He has brown eyes.

3 **Reflect** Think and color.

My project is ☆☆☆

I can make a poster and describe my friend.

 **Extra time?**

Tell your friend about your poster.

My progress journal

1 Look, read, and circle. Then ask and answer.

1 She has **long** / **short** hair.
She **can** / **can't** take pictures.

2 He has **blond** / **dark** hair.
He **can** / **can't** cook.

3 She has **curly** / **straight** hair.
She **can** / **can't** ride a scooter.

4 He's **tall** / **short**. He **can** / **can't** play basketball.

Is he tall or short?

He's short.

2 Draw your favorite character from the unit. Then circle and write.

This is _____.

He / **She** is _____.

He / **She** has _____.

He / **She** can _____.

3 Think and draw ☹, ☺, or 😄.

My favorite word from this unit is
_____.

14

Listening

1   **Listen and match.**

Lucy

Eva

Sam

Mark

May

Tom

Reading

2 **Read and put a** ✔ **or** ✘.

1
He has curly hair. ✘

2
He has a beard. ○

3
She can cook. ○

4
He can't horseback ride. ○

Speaking

3 **Look at 1. Answer the questions.**

💬 **Let's talk!**

1 How many trees can you see?
2 Who's tall?
3 Who has curly hair?
4 Describe your friend.

 Choose your favorite activity in the unit and stick.

2 At the ocean

Words I know	Words I want to learn
boat ocean octopus	_____
_____	_____
_____	_____

Video quiz

1 ▶ 2A **Watch again and do the quiz.**

1 🖉 **Read and match.**

ⓐ Dory

ⓑ Crush

ⓒ Marlin

ⓓ Destiny

1 helps Dory and Marlin.

2 is a nice shark.

3 asks a turtle for help.

4 can't find her mom and dad.

2 Check (✔). Who does Dory ask for help?

ⓐ

ⓑ

ⓒ

ⓓ

2 ✏️ **Choose and write.** | boat   ocean   octopus   shark |

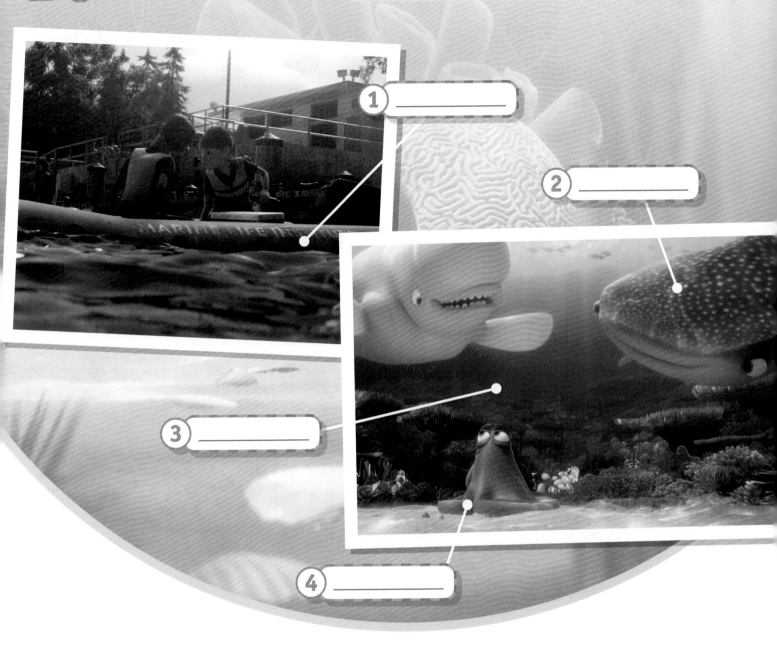

1 _____

2 _____

3 _____

4 _____

3 Challenge! ✏️ **Find and write. What animal is Crush?**

r u l e t

Crush is a t ___ ___ ___ ___ ___ .

I can name ocean words.

17

LESSON 2
Vocabulary

1 2.1 Listen and follow. Help Dory find her home.

start

finish

2 Look at 1. Choose and write.

crabs   dolphins   jellyfish   shells   starfish

1 The _____ are red.

2 There are six _____ .

3 There's one _____ .

4 There are three purple _____ .

5 There aren't any _____ .

Extra time?

Draw your favorite ocean animal. Write or tell a friend about it.

18

I can  name ocean animals and things on the beach.

1  **Listen and number.**

a

b

c

d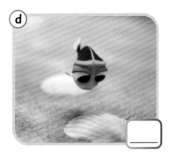

🧩 **Number and write.**

those? ☐   are ☐   What ☐

_____

2 ✏️ 💬 **Join the dots. Then ask and answer.**

What's that?

It's a …

What are those?

They're …

🕐 **Extra time?**

Look around your classroom. Ask or write two questions for your friend.

I can ask and answer about what things are.

The beach trip

1 Look and number in order.

a It's a starfish.

b Wow! Thanks, everyone.

c Oh, no! Look at the beach!

d There! Help us clean the beach.

2 Choose and write. When does Pedro ask for help and why?

Can you help me?   I can help this starfish alone.

1 _____

2 _____

3 Who's your favorite character? Check (✔).

 **1**

 **2**

 **3**

 **4**

I can read and understand a story.

Extra time?
Design a message for a beach clean-up.

1 ✏️ Read and match.

1 Amy has a surfboard.

2 James has an umbrella.

3 Nadia has a sunhat.

4 Brody has a towel.

5 Taylor has a bucket.

6 Caleb has a sandcastle.

Sing-along

2 ✏️ SB 2.10 Look, write, and match. Then listen and check. 🎵

surfboard   towel   sandcastle   sunhat

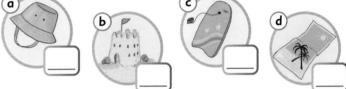

Let's go to the beach today

Make a 1 _____ , swim, and play!

  Is this your umbrella?

  Yes, it is! It's our umbrella.

Let's go to the beach today

Put a 2 _____ on, swim, and play!

  Are these your buckets?

  Yes, they are. They're our buckets.

Let's go to the beach today

Take a 3 _____ out, swim, and play!

  Is this your 4 _____ ?

  Yes, it is. It's our towel.

Let's go to the beach today

Make a sandcastle, swim, and play!

3 ✏️ Circle the odd one out.

1 octopus   whale   towel   sea lion

2 crab   bucket   dolphin   shark

3 umbrella   sunhat   shell   dolphin

🏠 English at home
Sing the song for your family!

I can   name things on the beach.

1  Read and circle.

1 Look! Is that **our / their** boat?

No, it isn't. They don't have a boat.

2 Look! Are those **their / our** surfboards?

Yes, they are! Quick! Swim!

3 Look! Is that **our / their** umbrella?

Yes. They can't catch it. Let's help them!

Number and write.

our ☐   Are ☐   towels? ☐   these ☐

_____

2 Look and write *our* or *their*.

1 Is this _____ new house?

Yes, it is. Let's go and see your room.

2 Are those _____ dogs?

Yes. They have six dogs!

3 It's Ava and Jon. Is that _____ mom?

No, it's their aunt.

22

I can ask and answer about possessions.

Extra time?

Write or ask two questions with *our* or *their*.

Asking for help

1 🖊 🎧 **Look, read, and match. Then listen and check.**

1 I can't see the board. Can you help me?   **2** Can you help me? I need that book.

3 This is hard. Can you help me, please?

$7 \times ? = 49$

2 💡 🖊 **Think about when you need help. Draw and write.**

When do you need help?

My portfolio

Who can you ask?

I can ask _____

_____ .

What can you say?

_____

_____

⭐ **Be a hero!** ⭐

Act out the scenes from 1 with a friend.

I can ask for help.

The awesome octopus

Life Science

1 Read and put a ✔ or ✘.

1 An octopus has bones. ◯

2 It has eight arms. ◯

3 It's weak. ◯

4 It doesn't have skin. ◯

5 It can change color. ◯

6 It can hide. ◯

2 🖊 Look. Then write sentences using *and*.

I can write

They're very strong. They have suckers on them.
  ↳ They're very strong and they have suckers on them.

1 Frogs can live in water. They can live in trees.
_____

2 Crabs can walk. They can swim.
_____

3 🖊 Draw an octopus and write your two favorite facts.

The octopus _____

_____

_____

_____

Extra time?

What other animals
don't have bones?
Find out!

I can understand and write about the octopus.

My ocean scene

1 (Create) **Think and complete. Then write and make your scene.**

Animal / Object:	crab		
Number:	2		
Color:	red and black		
Can it swim?	(yes) / no	yes / no	yes / no
Size:	big / (small)	big / small	big / small

My ocean scene

_____

_____

_____

_____

There are two crabs. They are red and black. They can swim. They are small.

2 **Look and check (✔). Then practice with a friend.**

Can the class hear you? Ask before you start.

1 I'm sorry. I can't hear you.

2 Can you hear me?

3 (Reflect) **Think and color.**

My project is ☆☆☆

I can make and present an ocean scene.

Extra time? Which ocean scene is your favorite? Why? Tell a friend.

25

My progress journal

1 💬 **Look, read, and put a ✔ or ✗. Then ask and answer.**

1 Pedro and Laura are on the beach. ◯

2 Their bucket is blue. ◯

3 There is a starfish on the umbrella. ◯

4 The surfboard is yellow. ◯

5 There are shells on the sandcastle. ◯

6 The towel is red and white. ◯

| What are these? | They're towels. |

2 ✏️ **Draw two ocean animals. Then circle and write.**

What are **these** / **those** ?

They're _____.

They can _____.

They have _____ bodies and

_____.

3 💡 ✏️ **Think and draw ☹, ☺, or 😄.**

 ◯    ◯    ◯    ◯

My favorite ocean word is

_____.

Listening

1 🎧 2.4 **Listen and check (✔).**

① What's on the beach?

ⓐ ⓑ ⓒ

② What's in the ocean?

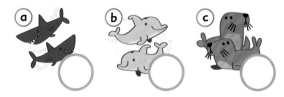

ⓐ ⓑ ⓒ

③ What's this?

ⓐ ⓑ ⓒ

④ What's on the towel?

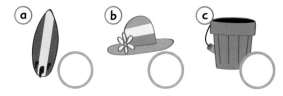

ⓐ ⓑ ⓒ

Reading

2 ✏️ **Read and write Yes or No.**

① There's a boat on the ocean.

_____No_____

② There are shells on the sandcastle.

_____

③ There's a surfboard on the towel.

_____

④ There are two whales.

_____

Speaking

3 💬 **Look at 2. Answer the questions.**

💬 **Let's talk!**

1 What color is the umbrella?
2 What's on the beach?
3 Talk about the ocean. What can you see?

 Choose your favorite activity in the unit and stick.

3 Around town

Words I know	Words I want to learn
truck tram street	_____
_____	_____
_____	_____

Video quiz

1 ▶ **3A** **Watch again and do the quiz.**

1 ✏️ Read and circle.

ⓐ Tadashi makes a **robot** / **train**.

ⓑ Hiro finds Baymax on the **street** / **house**.

ⓒ There are **planes** / **cars** on the street.

ⓓ There's a **red** / **blue** truck.

ⓔ Baymax is on the **tram** / **train**.

2 Check (✔). How does Hiro feel at the end?

2 ✏️ **Choose and write.**

> bus   street   tram   truck

1 _____

2 _____

3 _____

4 _____

3 Challenge! ✏️ **Follow and write. Where does Hiro's aunt work?**

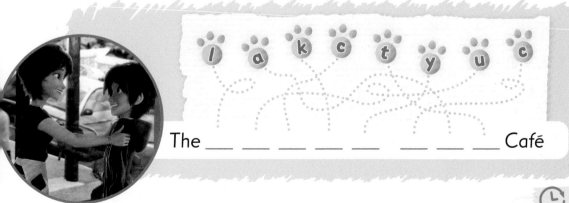

l   a   k   c   t   y   u   c

The ___ ___ ___ ___ ___ ___ ___ ___ Café

🕐 **Extra time?**

Close your books. Remember the pictures and say. There's a blue bus.

 **I can** I can name things on the street.

1 ✏️ Find and number.

a

b

c

d

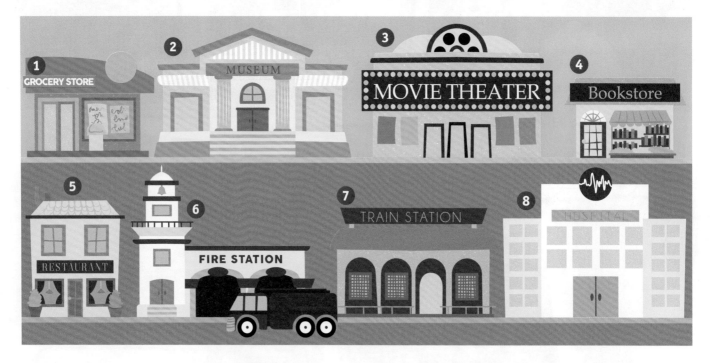

e

f

g

h

2 ✏️ Look at 1 and write.

1 The grocery store is next to the _____ .

2 There's a red truck at the _____ .

3 The _____ is small.

4 The _____ is next to the hospital.

5 The bookstore is next to the _____ .

6 The _____ is next to the fire station.

 I can name places in town.

🕐 **Extra time?**

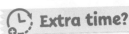
Draw your school.
Where is it? Write
or say.

1 🖊 **Look, read, and circle.**

1 Is there a tram?

Yes, there is. / No, there isn't.

2 Is there a movie theater?

Yes, there is. / No, there isn't.

3 Are there any cars?

Yes, there are. / No, there aren't.

4 Are there any buses?

Yes, there are. / No, there aren't.

🧩 **Number and write.**

any   there   Are   buses?

_____

2 🖊 **Look and write Is there or Are there. Then answer.**

1 _____Is there_____ a museum?

_____Yes, there is._____

2 _____ any buses?

_____

3 _____ a fire station?

_____

4 _____ any boats?

_____

⏰ **Extra time?**

What is the same or different about your town? Write or say.

I can ask and answer about places in town.

The treasure hunt

1 Match. Where do the clues lead?

❶ It's a station, but you can't see a train here.

ⓐ restaurant

❷ There's food here.

ⓑ movie theater

❸ You can see dinosaurs here.

ⓒ fire station

2 Look and write. How do they keep trying?

> bored   Don't give up!   tired   We can do it!

❶ Pedro is _____ .

❷ Amelia says:

" _____ "

❸ Amelia is _____ .

❹ Pedro says:

" _____ "

3 Do you like the story? Color.

I don't like it.   It's OK.   I like it.   I like it a lot.   I love it!

I can read and understand a story.

Extra time?

Write clues for these places.
bookstore   hospital

1 🎧 3.1 ✏️ **Listen and follow.**

2 ✏️ **Look at 1. Choose and write.**

apartment building   factory   hotel   mall   police station   sports center

1 There is a car next to it. _____

2 It's very tall. _____

3 You can swim there. _____

4 There are trees next to it. _____

5 It's next to the sports center. _____

6 It's big and gray. _____

3 ✏️ **Circle places in blue and transportation in green.**

grocery store   tram   police station   mall   hotel

factory   scooter   truck   hospital   bus

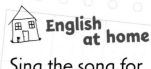

English at home
Sing the song for your family!

I can name places in town.

1 🎧 3.2 ✏️ **Listen and number. Where's Baymax?**

a

b

c

🧩 **Number and write.**

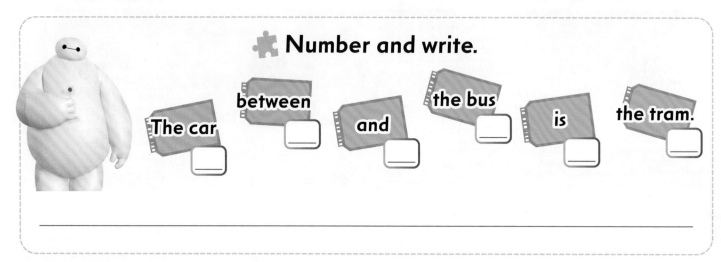

The car ___ between ___ and ___ the bus ___ is ___ the tram. ___

_____

2 ✏️ 💬 **Find, choose, and write. Then ask and answer.**

across from   behind   between   in front of

❶ The police station is _____ the mall.

❷ The man is _____ the grocery store.

❸ The bus is _____ the red car.

❹ The movie theater is _____ the mall and the school.

Where's the police station?

It's across from the mall.

 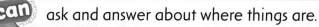 ask and answer about where things are.

🕐 **Extra time?**

Where do you sit in class? Write or say.

Keep trying!

1  **Look and number in order. Then listen, choose, and write.**

Don't give up!   I can do it!   I can't do it.

a _____

b This is hard!

_____

Look at me!

c

Good job!

_____

d I'm tired.

2   **Think. What's hard for you? Circle and write.**

 My portfolio

Sometimes I can't ...

do homework
play the piano
speak English
play a video game
_____

I say ...

I can't stop now!
Don't give up!
I can do it!
_____

Then ...

I **can** / **can't** do it!
I feel _____ .

☆ **Be a hero!** ☆

Act out the story
from 1.

I can keep trying.

3D shapes in a city

1 ✏️ **Join the dots. Then match.**

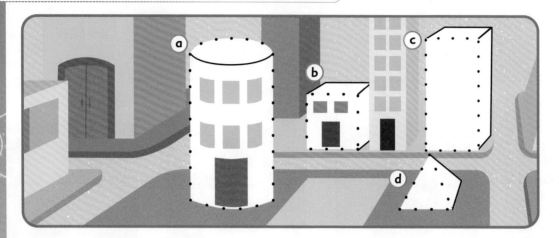

1 cube

2 pyramid

3 cylinder

4 cuboid

2 ✏️ **Look and circle describing words. Then add very.**

I can write

This hotel is a (tall) cylinder. → This hotel is a very tall cylinder.

1 This building is a small cube.

_____

2 I live in a nice apartment building.

_____

3 ✏️ **Design a building. Write about it using ideas in 2.**

This is a _____ .

It's _____

_____

_____ .

I can understand and write about 3D shapes.

🕐 **Extra time?**

Find examples of 3D shapes around you.

Self-management

My town poster

1 🖉 **Check (✔) and write places in your town. Then share the tasks.**

Say what you can do.
Share work.
Do your task.

school ◯   hospital ◯   factory ◯

police station ◯   grocery store ◯   mall ◯

movie theater ◯   _____ ◯   _____ ◯

My task: I can draw _____ .   _____ can draw _____ .

_____ can draw _____ .   _____ can draw _____ .

2 🖉 (Create) **Complete for your town. Then write and draw.**

The fire station is across from the movie theater.

My town

_____

_____

_____

_____

_____

_____

_____

3 🖉 (Reflect) **Think and color.**

Our project is ☆☆☆

🕒 **Extra time?**

Tell your friend about your town.

I can make a poster and write about my town.

37

My progress journal

1 🖊 Look, read, and circle.

1. There **is** / **isn't** an apartment building.

2. The bike is **behind** / **in front of** the restaurant.

3. There are two **cars** / **buses**.

4. The bookstore is **across from** / **between** the grocery store and the restaurant.

GROCERY

BOOK STORE

RESTAURANT

MOVIE THEATER

2 🖊 Draw a cat in the picture in 1. Then answer.

1. Where's the cat? _____

2. Where's Amelia? _____

3. Is there a bus? _____

4. Are there any scooters? _____

3 💡 🖊 Think and draw ☹, ☺, or 😀.

My favorite city word is

_____.

38

Listening

1   **Listen and color.**

Reading

2 **Look and write.**

crutk   tipholas   mart   setboroko   cotrfay

1 <u>t r u c k</u>   **2** ___ ___ ___ ___ ___ ___ ___ ___

3 ___ ___ ___ ___   **4** ___ ___ ___ ___ ___ ___ ___ ___ ___

5 ___ ___ ___ ___ ___ ___ ___

Speaking

3 **Add to the picture in 1 and say.**
Then talk about the picture.

There's a …

There are …

It's between …

 Choose your favorite activity in the unit and stick.

4 Let's eat

Words I know	Words I want to learn
cake peas soup	_____
_____	_____
_____	_____

▶ Video quiz

1 ▶ **Watch again and do the quiz.**

1 Read and circle.

ⓐ Who helps make the soup?

ⓑ What's in the soup?

ⓒ Who likes Tiana's soup?

ⓓ Who likes Tiana's cake?

2 Look and write.

Tiana can _____ .

2 Choose and write.

cake   peas   potatoes   soup

1 _____

2 _____

3 _____

4 _____

3 Challenge! Circle. Who's Charlotte?

Charlotte is Tiana's **sister** / **mother** / **friend**.

Extra time?

Circle the food words.

potatoescakepeassoup

I can name food.

1 ✏️ **Look and number.**

1	2	3	4

5	6	7	8

ⓐ pineapples ☐   ⓑ mangoes ☐   ⓒ lemons ☐

ⓓ chicken ☐   ⓔ nuts ☐   ⓕ kiwis ☐

ⓖ yogurt ☐   ⓗ chocolate ☐

2 ✏️ **Look, choose, and write.**

chocolate   kiwis   lemons   mango
nut   pineapple

❶ The head is a _____ .

❷ The nose is a _____ .

❸ The eyes are _____ .

❹ The mouth is a _____ .

❺ The ears are _____ .

❻ On each ear, there is _____ .

🕒 **Extra time?**

Which food in 1 do you like? Write or tell a friend.

I can name food.

1 🖊 Look, read, and circle.

1. Sara **likes** / **doesn't like** yogurt.
2. She **likes** / **doesn't like** mangoes, too.
3. Her brother **likes** / **doesn't like** yogurt or mangoes.
4. He **doesn't like** / **loves** chocolate!

🧩 **Number and write.**

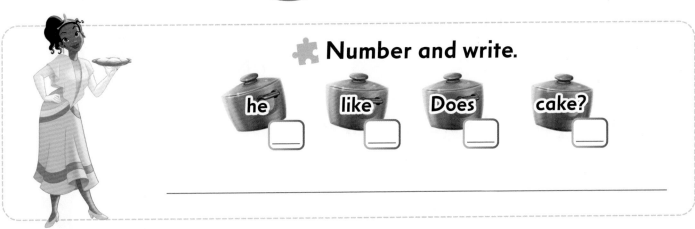

he   like   Does   cake?

_____

2 🖊 Follow and answer.

1. Does Sylvie like chicken?

_____

2. Does she like pineapples?

_____

3. Does Ryan like cake?

_____

4. Does he like nuts?

_____

5. Does Emma like lemons?

_____

6. Does she like kiwis?

_____

Sylvie   Ryan   Emma

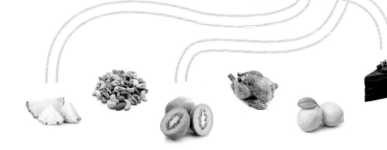

⏱ **Extra time?**

What food does your friend like? Ask and write or draw.

I can say what people like and don't like.

43

Let's make some juice!

1 ✏️ Read and write.

1 _____ can make chocolate cookies.

2 _____ can't cook. He can draw.

3 _____ can ride a bike. He can't cook.

4 _____ can make juice.

 Laura

 Pedro

 Niko

 Will

2 ✏️ Draw you in the story. Then write.

I can help! I can _____ .

3 💡 Who's your favorite character? Check (✔).

 1

 2

 3

 4

 5

I can read and understand a story.

Extra time?

What fruit do you put in your juice? Write, draw, or say.

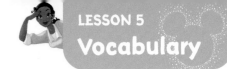

1 🖊 🎧 **Look and match. Then listen and number.**

 a

 b

c

Sing-along

2 🖊 🎵 **Read, choose, and write. Then listen and check.**

> breakfast   burger   cereal   dinner   fries   lunch

I'm hungry. What's for ① _____ ?   Yogurt and ④ _____ . That's breakfast.

I'm hungry. What's for ② _____ ?   Bread and jam. That's lunch!

I'm hungry. What's for ③ _____ ?   ⑤ _____ and ⑥ _____ .

I'm hungry. Munch, munch, munch!   That's dinner.

Now some chocolate. Munch, munch, munch!

3 🖊 **Circle the odd one out.**

① chicken   kiwis   lemons

② mangoes   pineapples   peas

③ chocolate   potatoes   cake

④ breakfast   restaurant   lunch

English at home

Sing the song for
your family!

I can name food and meals.

1 🎧 4.2 ✏️ **Listen and circle.**

① What would you like?
I'd like some chicken, **please** / **thank you**.

② Would you like some fries?
No, thank you. / **Yes, please.**

③ Would you like some juice?
No, thank you. / **Yes, please.**

🧩 **Number and write.**

like ☐   you ☐   food? ☐   Would ☐   some ☐

_____

2 💬 **Check (✔) for you. Then ask and check (✔) for your friend.**

Me

My friend

What would you like?   I'd like some fries, please.

⏰ **Extra time?**

What would you like for breakfast?
Write or say.

I can ask and answer about what food I would like.

Recognizing strengths

1 🖊 **Look, read, and match.**

1 I can help! I can climb.

2 I can paint. I'm good at it.

3 I can't play the piano, but I can sing.

4 I can play the piano. Then you can sing!

5 I can't sing, but I can dance.

2 💡 🖊 **Think about what you can do. Then write and say.**

My portfolio

What can you do?

I can _____ _____ .

How can you use it?

I can _____ _____ .

I can read. I can read stories to my baby brother.

⭐Be a hero!⭐
Who can you help today? How?

I can say what I'm good at.

47

Food groups

1 ✏️ **Circle the food in the correct color. Write one more in each group.**

carbohydrates   fats   proteins   fruit and vegetables   dairy

(nuts)   (peas ___)   (chicken ___)   (yogurt ___)   (bread ___)

2 ✏️ **Look. Then add commas (,) to separate words in a list.**

I can write

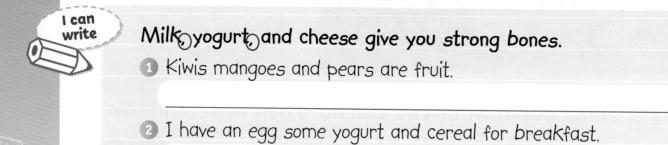

Milk, yogurt, and cheese give you strong bones.

1 Kiwis mangoes and pears are fruit.

_____

2 I have an egg some yogurt and cereal for breakfast.

_____

3 💡 ✏️ **Design a picnic lunch with all five food groups. Draw and write.**

For my lunch, I'd like

_____

_____

_____ .

🕒 **Extra time?**

Tell a friend about your picnic lunch.

I can understand and write about food groups.

Presentation

My food menu

1 Create **Think and check (✔) for your menu. Then create your menu.**

breakfast ✔		lunch ✔		dinner ✔	
burger ○	cereal ○	chicken ○	eggs ○
fries ○	peas ○	potatoes ○	cake ○
yogurt ✔	milk ○	oranges ○	rice ○
kiwis ○	nuts ○	chocolate ○	soup ○

FOOD MENU
Breakfast

Lunch

Dinner

2 **Which picture shows good role-playing? Check (✔). Then practice with a friend.**

Listen to your friend.
Take turns.
Say *please* and *thank you*.

a

Would you like some soup?

Yes, please.

b

Would you like some ...?

I'd like some ... .

3 Reflect **Think and color.**

My project is ☆☆☆

Extra time?

Which project do you like best? Tell a friend.

I can make a menu and act out a scene.

49

My progress journal

1 Read and color. What does Niko like?

Niko likes mangoes. He likes yogurt for breakfast, but he doesn't like cereal.

For lunch, he likes a burger.

For dinner, he likes chicken and fries. He doesn't like potatoes or peas. Oh, and he likes cake, too!

2 What would you like from Niko's table in 1? Circle and write. Then play with a friend.

I'd like _____

_____ .

Would you like some peas?   Yes, please.

3 Think and draw ☹, ☺, or 😄.

My favorite food word is

_____ .

Listening

1 Listen and write.

1 What's the boy's name? _____Dan_____

2 How old is he? _____

3 How many sandwiches does he have? _____

4 Who has yogurt for breakfast? _____

5 What time is it? _____ o'clock

Reading

2 Read and write *Yes* or *No*.

1 Tom has chicken and fries.

_____Yes_____

2 Lucy has mangoes.

_____

3 Tom has yogurt.

_____

4 Lucy has peas.

_____

Speaking

3 Look at 2. Point and say. Then answer the questions for you.

 Let's talk!

1 What would you like?
2 Who likes these foods in your family?
3 Do you eat lunch in school?
4 What's your favorite sandwich?

 Choose your favorite activity in the unit and stick.

5 The weather

Words I know	Words I want to learn
summer winter fall	_____
_____	_____
_____	_____

▶ Video quiz

1 ▶ **5A Watch again and do the quiz.**

1 ✏️ Read and write *Yes* or *No*.

 a

b

 c

 d

ⓐ It's winter.   _____

ⓑ The ants work hard.   _____

ⓒ The ants can climb.   _____

ⓓ Flik has a lot of ideas.   _____

2 ✏️ Read and circle.

 a

 b

The ants **like** / **don't like** Flik's ideas.

Dot **likes** / **doesn't like** Flik's ideas.

2 🖊 **Choose and write.**

| fall | spring | summer | winter |

1 _____

2 _____

3 _____

4 _____

3 Challenge! 🖊 **Find and write. What animal is Heimlich?**

a	c	e	i	l	p	r	t
1	2	3	4	5	6	7	8

Heimlich is a

___ ___ ___ ___ ___ ___ ___ ___ ___ ___ ___ .
2   1   8   3   7   6   4   5   5   1   7

⏰ **Extra time?**

Close your books.
Use new words in
a sentence.
My birthday is in winter.

I can name the seasons.

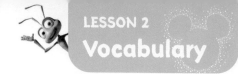

1 🎧 5.1 ✏️ **Listen and number.**

a

b ____

c ____

d ____

2 ✏️ **Look and put a ✔ or ✗. Then write.**

cool ✔   cloudy ◯

warm ◯   rainy ◯

snowy ◯   stormy ◯

sunny ◯   windy ◯

1 It's _____cool_____ , _____ ,

_____ , and _____ .

2 It isn't _____ , _____ ,

_____ , or _____ .

🕐 **Extra time?**

Write or tell a friend about your favorite weather.

It's warm. It isn't stormy.

54

I can describe the weather.

1 🖊 **Look, read, and write *Yes* or *No*.**

ⓐ It's cold and rainy. _____

ⓑ It's very sunny. _____

ⓐ It's very windy. _____

ⓑ It's warm and sunny. _____

🧩 **Number and write.**

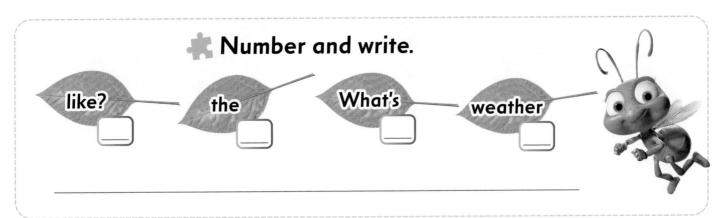

like? ☐ the ☐ What's ☐ weather ☐

_____

2 🖊 **What's the weather like? Look, choose, and write. Then draw the weather today and write.**

snowy   very (x2)   warm

ⓐ It's _____ cold.

ⓑ It's cold and

_____ .

ⓐ It's sunny and

_____ .

ⓑ It's _____ sunny.

It's _____ .

_____

🕐 **Extra time?**

Show your picture to a friend.

 ask and answer about the weather.

55

The kite

1 🖊 **Read and circle.**

❶ It's **windy** / **cool**.

❷ The table **is** / **isn't** next to the tree.

❸ The **ball** / **kite** is in the tree.

❹ **Two** / **Four** friends pull the kite from the tree.

2 **Read and check (✔). What do they say?**

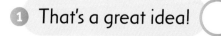
❶ That's a great idea! ◯

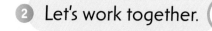
❷ Let's work together. ◯

❸ I don't like your idea! ◯

❹ Good job! ◯

3 💡 🖊 **Which idea do you like? Circle.**

❶

❷

❸

❹

Extra time?

Can you think of another idea to get the kite?

I can read and understand a story.

1 🎧 5.2 ✏️ **Listen and match.**

   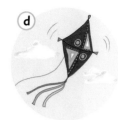

Joe

Kate

2 ✏️ **Look at 1. Choose and write.**

fly   go   indoors   make   plant   sledding

1. In spring, Joe and his friends _____ to the park.
   They _____ seeds and they _____ a kite.

2. In winter, Kate and her sister _____ snowballs and they go
   _____ . They play _____ , too.

3 ✏️ **Write more activities.**

summer   both   winter

swim in the ocean   go to the park   make snowballs

_____   _____   _____

_____   _____   _____

English at home
Sing the song for
your family!

I can   name seasonal activities.

57

1  **Listen and check (✔). What do the children do in summer?**

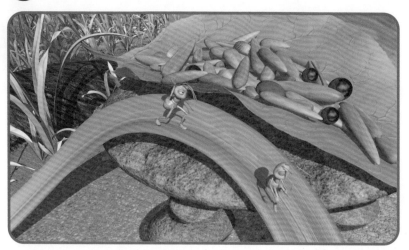

1 go to the park ⭕

2 work hard ⭕

3 go to school ⭕

4 fly kites ⭕

5 ride their scooters ⭕

6 play indoors ⭕

🧩 **Number and write.**

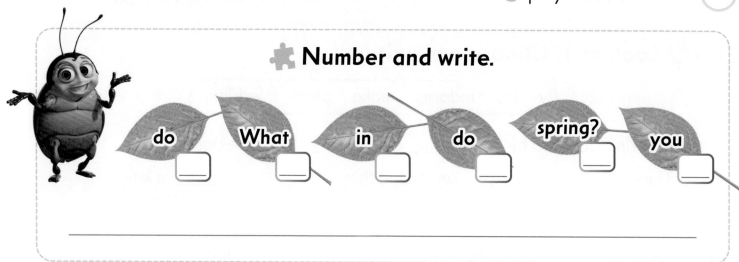

do ☐   What ☐   in ☐   do ☐   spring? ☐   you ☐

_____

2 ✏️ 💬 **Write. What do you do in spring and fall? Then ask and answer.**

spring

fall

What do you do in spring?

We play soccer.

🕐 **Extra time?**

What do you do in winter? Write or tell a friend.

I can   ask and answer about seasonal activities.

Sharing ideas

1 ✏️ **Look and match.**

ⓐ Good idea!
Let's do it!

ⓑ OK. Let's plant
carrots and peas!

ⓒ Let's plant
carrot seeds.

ⓓ I don't like carrots.
Can we plant peas?

2 ✏️ **Read and check (✔). Then draw the last picture.**

My portfolio

1

Let's add nuts to
our cookies.

I don't like nuts. Can
we add chocolate?

2

Oh, OK. We can
add chocolate.

ⓐ

ⓑ

No, I want nuts!

3

⭐ **Be a hero!** ⭐
Act out the story
from 1.

I can listen to ideas and work together with others.

Life Science — Ant life

1 ✏️ **Read and circle. Then choose and write.**

a _____

bark   leaves   nest

1 Ants find food in **winter** / **summer** and fall.

2 In **winter** / **spring**, they sleep.

b _____

3 They work **alone** / **in teams** to build nests.

4 They can build their nests **underground** / **under water**.

c _____

2 ✏️ **Look and circle the words to contract. Then rewrite the sentences.**

(It is) warm in their nests. = It's warm in their nests.

I can write

1 It is cold in winter. _____

2 What is the weather like? _____

3 💡 ✏️ **Choose a season. Draw and write about the ants' life.**

It _____ . The ants _____ .

I can understand and write about the life of an ant.

🕐 **Extra time?**

What other animals sleep in winter? Find out!

My activity tree

1 Look, read, and match.

ⓐ I can show it to the class!

ⓑ I work on the project. I check my spelling.

ⓒ I think and plan my project.

ⓓ Then I prepare my things.

Plan your project.
Get your things.
Work on your project.
Check your spelling.
Show your project.

2 (Create) Check (✔) for your activity tree. Then write and draw. Make sure to check your spelling!

go sledding ◯

swim in the ocean ◯

play indoors ◯

fly a kite ◯

plant seeds ◯

In summer,
_____
_____ .

In fall,
_____
_____ .

In spring,
_____
_____ .

In winter,
_____
_____ .

◯ make snowballs

◯ go to the park

◯ ride a scooter

◯ _____

◯ _____

In spring, I plant seeds.

3 (Reflect) Think and color.

 My project is ☆ ☆ ☆

🕐 **Extra time?**

Tell your friend about your project.

 make and describe an activity tree.

My progress journal

1  **Look, read, and match.**

It's cold and snowy.
I make snowballs.

It's stormy and rainy.
I play indoors.

It's sunny and windy.
I fly a kite.

2 **Draw and write about your favorite season.**

1 What's your favorite season?
I like _____ .

2 What's the weather like?
_____

3 What do you wear?
_____

4 What do you and your friends do?
_____

3 **Think and draw ☹, ☺, or 😀.**

My favorite word
in this unit is
_____ .

Listening

1  **Listen and write.**

1. What's the girl's name? _____Kim_____
2. What number is her house? _____
3. What's the name of the park? _____ Park
4. What's the name of her cat? _____
5. How many cats do they have? _____

Reading

2 **Read and write.**

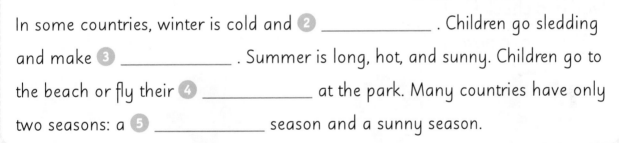

There are four seasons: spring, summer,
1 _____fall_____ , and winter.

In some countries, winter is cold and 2 _____ . Children go sledding
and make 3 _____ . Summer is long, hot, and sunny. Children go to
the beach or fly their 4 _____ at the park. Many countries have only
two seasons: a 5 _____ season and a sunny season.

rainy   plane   ~~fall~~   kites   sunny   snowballs   umbrella   snowy

Speaking

3 **Answer the questions for you.**

Let's talk!

1 What's your favorite season?
2 What's the weather like today?
3 What do you do in summer?
4 What do you do on rainy days?

 Choose your favorite activity in the unit and stick.

6 My day

Phrases I know

watch TV   go to school
do homework

_____

_____

Phrases I want to learn

_____

_____

_____

Video quiz

1 ▶ **6A** **Watch again and do the quiz.**

① Read and check (✔).

ⓐ Who has a new job?

ⓑ Who goes to school by bus?

ⓒ Who can't do his homework?

ⓓ Who listens to a story before bed?

② 🖉 Circle. How do the children help at home?

They **cook and clean** / **go to school.**

64

2 ✏️ Choose and write.

| do homework   go to school   go to work   watch TV |

1 _____

2 _____

3 _____

4 _____

3 Challenge! ✏️ Find and write. How does Mom go to work?

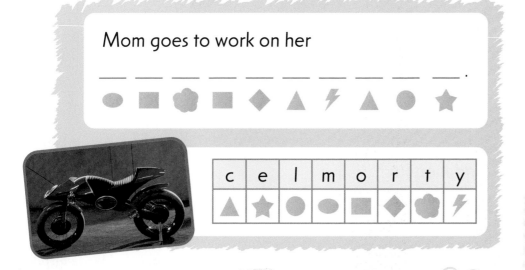

Mom goes to work on her

___ ___ ___ ___ ___ ___ ___ ___ ___ ___ .

⬤ ◼ ⬣ ◼ ◆ ▲ ⚡ ▲ ⬤ ★

c	e	l	m	o	r	t	y
▲	★	⬤	⬤	◼	◆	⬣	⚡

🕐 Extra time?

Say the new activities.
Do you do these things
every day?
Say Yes or No.

I can name daily routines.

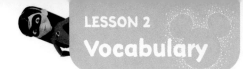
1 Listen and number.

2 Look at 1. Choose and write.

clean   come   exercise   go   pack   talk   wash   watch

1 I _____ home. Then I _____ up my room.

2 I _____ and then I _____ to my friends.

3 I _____ TV and then I _____ to bed.

4 I _____ my backpack. Then I _____ my face.

Extra time?

What time do you wake up? Write or tell a friend.

I can name daily routines.

1 ✏️ **Read and circle Yes or No.**

1 They have breakfast with their mom.
Yes / No

2 Dad and Jack-Jack watch TV.
Yes / No

3 Dad and Dash do homework.
Yes / No

4 Mom and Dad go to work.
Yes / No

🧩 **Number and write.**

 watch ☐

 they ☐

 TV? ☐

 Do ☐

_____

2 ✏️ **Look and write Yes, they do or No, they don't.**

Evie and Jim's afternoon activities!

1 Do they clean up their rooms? _____

2 Do they ride their bikes? _____

3 Do they do their homework? _____

4 Do they talk to their friends? _____

5 Do they exercise? _____

6 Do they watch TV? _____

 ⏱️ **Extra time?**

Ask or write two questions
for your friend.
Do you clean up your room?

I can ask and answer about daily routines.

Let's clean up!

1 ✏️ **Number in order.**

ⓐ Mom and Dad go to work. ☐　　ⓑ The children watch TV. ☐

ⓒ Dad comes home. ☐　　ⓓ They all help clean up. ☐

CLEAN THE HOUSE!

2 ✏️ **Check (✔). How do the children help? Then write how you help at home.**

ⓐ clean up ◯　　ⓑ read stories ◯

ⓒ do homework ◯　　ⓓ cook dinner ◯

_____

_____

_____

3 💡 ✏️ **Do you like the story? Color.**

I don't like it.　It's OK.　I like it.　I like it a lot.　I love it!

I can read and understand a story.

🕐 **Extra time?**
Make a list of people who help you at home.

1 Read and match.

ⓐ We go to sleep   ⓑ We do our homework   ⓒ We wake up   ⓓ We come home from school and play

in the morning.   at night.   in the afternoon.   in the evening.

Sing-along

2 SB 6.11 Read, choose, and write. Then listen and check.

at night   in the afternoon   in the evening   in the morning   on the weekend

I wake up ① _____ 🎵
And I go to school.
I do homework ② _____
And I clean up my room. 🎵

We have dinner ③ _____ ,
Then I watch TV.
I go to bed ④ _____ 🎵
And I go to sleep.

🎵 ⑤ _____ it's different. We have fun, fun, fun.

We go to the park. And play games in the sun, sun, sun!

3 Think and write. What do you do in the afternoon?

afternoon

do homework

English at home

Sing the song for your family!

I can use simple time expressions.

69

1  Listen and number.

a

b

c

d

🧩 **Number and write.**

you

do

up?

When

clean

_____

2 🖊 **Complete for you.**

activity	watch TV	do my homework	pack my backpack	clean up	exercise
❶ me	evening				
❷ my friend	afternoon				

3 💬 🖊 **Ask a friend and write in 2.**

When do you watch TV?

I watch TV in the afternoon.

I don't watch TV in the afternoon.
I watch TV in the evening.

⏱ **Extra time?**

What do you do on the weekend?

I can ask and answer about daily routines.

Helping at home

1 🖊 **Look and circle. Who's helping?**

Let's make dinner.

I can help with your homework.

Can you read me a story?

2 🖊 💬 **Read, look at 1, and number. Then say.**

ⓐ No, I'm tired. ☐   ⓑ Thank you. ☐   ⓒ Yes! I can help you. ☐

3 🖊 **Draw you helping at home and write.**

My portfolio

I help _____ .

☆ Be a hero! ☆

Who helps you at home? Make a "thank you" card.

I can help at home.

71

Science

Night and day

1 🖊️ **Read and match.**

1

Earth

2

Sun

3

Moon

ⓐ I can see it in the afternoon.

ⓑ I can see it at night.

ⓒ I live here.

ⓓ It takes 24 hours to spin around.

2 🖊️ **Look and circle. Then write sentences with *It*.**

I can write

Earth is big and round. (Earth) spins around.
↳ Earth is big and round. It spins around.

1 Where's the Moon? The Moon's behind a cloud.
_____

2 We live on Earth. Earth is big.
_____

3 💡 🖊️ **Draw your favorite time of day. Then circle and write.**

My favorite time of the day is the
morning / **afternoon** / **evening** /
night.

Is it light or dark? _____

Can you see the Moon? _____

Extra time?

Tell your friend about your favorite time of day. What can you do?

 I can understand and write about day and night.

Presentation

My activities clock

1 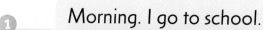 (Create) **Match for your activities clock. Then write and draw.**

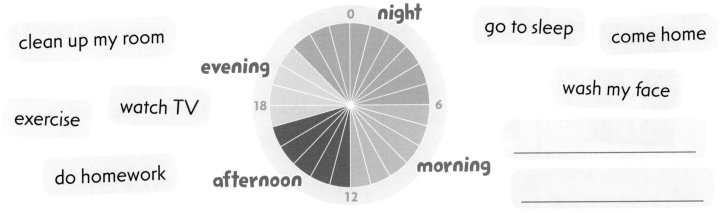

clean up my room

evening

exercise   watch TV

do homework   afternoon

night

go to sleep   come home

wash my face

_____

_____

morning

My day _____

I wake up at seven o'clock in the morning.

Point at the clock.
Say the times.
Speak slowly.

2 **Check (✔). How can you present your project? Then practice with a friend.**

① Morning. I go to school.

② I go to school at eight o'clock in the morning.

3 (Reflect) **Think and color.**

My project is ☆☆☆

Extra time?
Which activities clock is your favorite?
Tell a friend.

I can   design an activities clock and describe my day.

My progress journal

1 ✏️ Look, read, and circle.

1 I'm a doctor. I don't go to sleep at night. I **go to work** / **come home**!

2 I **clean up my room** / **exercise** in the afternoon.

3 I work in a factory. I work at night and I **wake up** / **come home** in the morning.

4 I **watch TV** / **pack my backpack** in the evening.

2 ✏️ What do you do on the weekend? Draw and answer.

1 When do you have breakfast?

_____

2 Do you watch TV in the afternoon?

_____

3 When do you go to sleep?

_____

3 💡 ✏️ Think and draw ☹️, 🙂, or 😄.

 ◯
 ◯
 ◯
 ◯

My favorite phrase in this unit is

_____.

74

Listening

1 🎧 **Listen and check (✓).**

① When do Pat and her brother go to school?

 a   b   c ✓

② What does Pat do in the afternoon?

 a   b   c

③ What do Ben and his family do in the evening?

 a   b   c

④ What does Ben do on the weekend?

 a   b   c

Reading

2 ✏️ **Look, read, and write.**

① What's the weather like on Saturday?
It's ____rainy____ .

② What do they do in the morning?
They _____ up.

③ Where do they go in the evening?
To the movie _____ .

④ What do they eat for dinner?
They eat _____ .

Speaking

3 💬 **Answer the questions for you.**

What time do you wake up?

What do you do when you come home from school?

What do you do on the weekend?

 Choose your favorite activity in the unit and stick.

7 At work

Video quiz

1 **Watch again and do the quiz.**

1 🖉 Read and circle.

Judy's parents are
farmers / bakers.

Judy goes to a
police / clerk school.

Judy **can / can't**
run fast.

2 Check (✔). What's Judy's dream job?

2 ✏️ Choose and write.

> baker   clerk   farmer   police officer

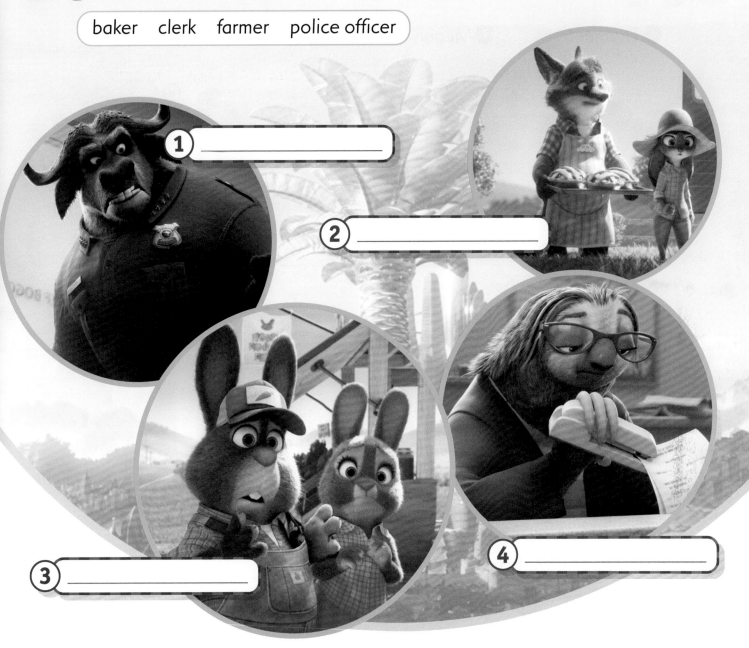

1 _____

2 _____

3 _____

4 _____

3 Challenge! ✏️ Follow and write. What's the lion's job?

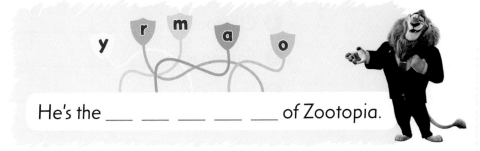

y   r   m   a   o

He's the ___ ___ ___ ___ ___ of Zootopia.

(L) **Extra time?**

Do you know people who do these jobs? Write or tell a friend. My uncle is a police officer.

I can name jobs.

77

1 🎧 7.1 ✏️ Listen and match.

❶ Thomas   **❷ Megan**   **❸ Fatima**   **❹ Eliot**

❺ Rosa   **❻ Liam**   **❼ Olivia**   **❽ Connor**

2 ✏️ Look at 1. Choose and write.

> architect   astronaut   athlete   bus driver   construction worker
> doctor   firefighter   vet

❶ Rosa is an _____ .

❷ Connor is a _____ .

❸ Megan is an _____ .

❹ Olivia is an _____ .

❺ Eliot is a _____ .

❻ Fatima is a _____ .

❼ Thomas is a _____ .

❽ Liam is a _____ .

Extra time?

What other jobs do you know? Say or write.

I can name jobs.

1  **Read and match.**

1 She doesn't want to be a doctor. She wants to be an astronaut. ☐

2 She doesn't want to be an athlete. She wants to be a police officer. ☐

3 He doesn't want to be a firefighter. He wants to be a clerk. ☐

 🧩 **Number and write.**

 do ☐ want ☐ What ☐ to ☐ be? ☐ you ☐

_____

2 ✏️ **Look and write.**

1

2

3

4

1 He _____ wants to be _____ a construction worker.

2 She _____ a vet.

3 _____ a clerk.

4 _____ an athlete.

⏰ **Extra time?**

Ask a friend. What do you want to be?

I can ask and answer about jobs.

The firefighter

1 ✏️ Look and number in order.

a — I can't find a picture of a firefighter.

b — I want to be a firefighter, too.

Fantastic! Dream big and work hard!

c — Pedro wants to be a teacher and I want to be an astronaut.

d — Look! There's a fire truck!

2 ✏️ Read and circle.

1. Laura wants to be a **firefighter** / **doctor**.
2. A firefighter **works** / **doesn't work** hard.
3. Laura's dream is **small** / **big**.

3 💡 Who's your favorite character? Check (✔).

1
2
3
4
5
6

I can read and understand a story.

1 ✏️ Look, read, and match.

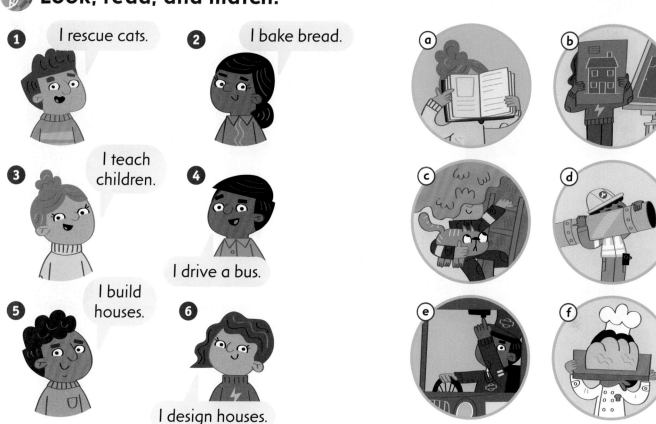

1 I rescue cats.
2 I bake bread.
3 I teach children.
4 I drive a bus.
5 I build houses.
6 I design houses.

a b c d e f

2 ✏️ Look at 1. Choose and write.

bake   ~~build~~   design   drive   rescue   teach

1 Construction workers build houses.
2 _____ bread.
3 _____ cats.
4 _____ children.
5 _____ buses.
6 _____ houses.

3 ✏️ Circle the odd one out.

1 drive   draw   tram   play

2 clerk   astronaut   rescue   construction worker

3 help   baker   ride   teach

4 design   build   bus driver   bake

English at home

Sing the song for your family!

I can say what people do at work.

1 🎧 7.2 ✏️ **Listen and number.**

a

b

c

🧩 **Number and write.**

he

What

do?

does

_____

2 ✏️ 💬 **Read, choose, and write. Then ask and answer.**

bake   build   drive   ~~teach~~

1 She ____teaches____ at the police school.

2 Gideon _____ cakes and bread.

3 He _____ houses.

4 Judy _____ a police car.

What does he or she do?

She drives a police car.

 ask and answer about people's jobs.

⏲️ **Extra time?**

Write or tell a friend about someone in your family.

Dreaming big

1 🖉 **Look, read, and match. What are their dreams?**

ⓐ learn to horseback ride

ⓑ have a cat

ⓒ play soccer with friends

ⓓ be a baker

2 🖉 💡 **Write and draw. How can you make your dream come true?**

My portfolio

1 My dream is to _____ .

2 I dream _____ .

3 I make my dream come true. I can _____ .

⭐ **Be a hero!** ⭐

Talk to a friend about his/her dreams.

I can dream big.

Technology

Robots at work

1 ✏️ **Circle the robots. Who do they help? Match.**

ⓐ It helps a family.

ⓑ It helps firefighters.

ⓒ It helps doctors.

2 ✏️ **Look. Then combine the sentences with *or*.**

I can write

Robots don't feel tired. They don't feel bored.
↳ Robots don't feel tired or bored.

① Robots can't make friends. They can't play soccer.
_____

② I don't like fall. I don't like winter.
_____

3 💡 ✏️ **Design a robot. Draw and write.**

My robot can work in _____ .

It can _____ and _____ .

It can't _____

_____ .

🕐 **Extra time?**

Where else can robots work?

  understand and write about how robots help people.

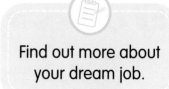

My dream job poster

1 ✏️ **Choose and write. Then check (✔) how you can find out about your dream job.**

Find out more about your dream job.

| read a book   talk to someone   use a computer |

_____   _____   _____

2 ✏️ (Create) **Think and complete. Then write and draw.**

My dream job

I want to be **a / an** _____ .

I want to work **inside / outside** at a

restaurant ◯   farm ◯   police station ◯

hospital ◯   fire station ◯   _____ ◯

When?

◯ ◯ ◯ ◯

_____
_____
_____
_____

My dream job is a doctor. A doctor works at a hospital.

3 ✏️ (Reflect) **Think and color.**

My project is ☆☆☆

 I can make a poster about my dream job.

Extra time?
Which project do you like best? Why? Write or say.

85

My progress journal

1 ✏️ Look, read, and circle.

❶ Daisy **wants** / **doesn't want** to be an astronaut.

❷ Tom **wants** / **doesn't want** to be a farmer.

❸ Will **wants** / **doesn't want** to be a baker.

❹ Pedro **wants** / **doesn't want** to be an athlete.

❺ Amelia **wants** / **doesn't want** to a firefighter.

2 ✏️ Draw someone you know doing their job. Then write and circle.

❶ Who's this? This is _____ .

❷ What's his/her job?

He's / **She's** _____ .

❸ What does he/she do every day?

He / **She** _____ .

3 💡 ✏️ Think and draw ☹, ☺, or 😄.

My favorite job word is

_____ .

Listening

1   **Listen and match.**

Sue

Grace

Steve

Matt

Anna

Reading

2 **Read and write.**

vet

astronaut

~~teacher~~

clerk

bus

truck

baker

doctor

What do you want to be? Do you want to work indoors?

A **1** ___teacher___ teaches children indoors and a **2** _____ works

at a computer. Do you want to work outdoors? You can be a firefighter

and drive a red **3** _____ . Do you like animals? A **4** _____

works with animals. Can you cook? You can be a **5** _____ or you

can work in a restaurant. There are a lot of great jobs!

Speaking

3 **Answer the questions for you.**

Do you want to be a teacher?

What do you want to be?

Do you like animals?

Can you cook?

⭐ **Choose your favorite activity in the unit and stick.**

8 After school

Phrases I know	Phrases I want to learn
collect shells	_____
buy ice cream	_____
_____	_____
_____	

Video quiz

1  **Watch again and do the quiz.**

1 Read and check (✔).

ⓐ Who's scared of Stitch?

ⓑ Who wants to collect shells?

ⓒ Who goes on a ride with Lilo?

2 Read and circle. Why is Lilo happy?

ⓐ Stitch is nice.

ⓑ Stitch is mean.

2 🖊 **Choose and write.**

> buy ice cream   collect shells   go on a ride   listen to music

1 _____

2 _____

3 _____

4 _____

3 **Challenge!** 🖊 **Follow and write. Where do Nani and Lilo find Stitch?**

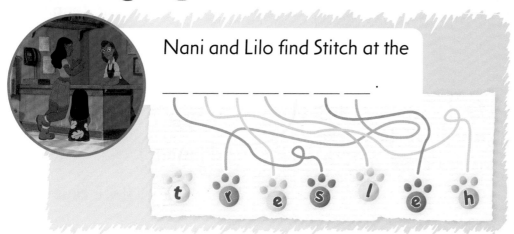

Nani and Lilo find Stitch at the

_ _ _ _ _ _ _ _ _ _ .

t   r   e   s   l   e   h

🕒 **Extra time?**

Close your books.
Act out and say the
free-time activities.

I can name free-time activities.

89

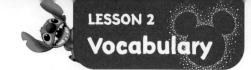

1 🖋 **Follow and find. Then write S (Sofia) or H (Hassan).**

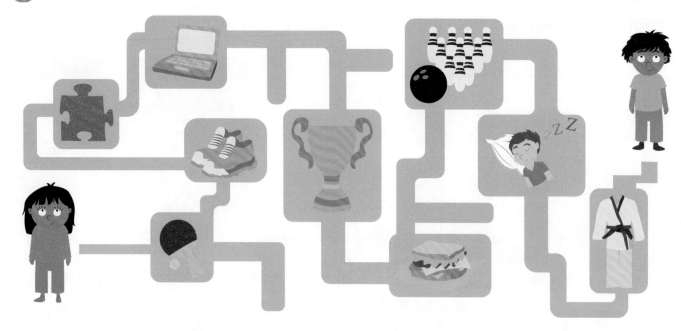

❶ I do a jigsaw puzzle. ☐

❸ I bowl with my friends. ☐

❺ I have a picnic. ☐

❼ I surf the internet. ☐

❷ I do judo. ☐

❹ I go for a walk. ☐

❻ I play table tennis. ☐

❽ I take a nap. ☐

2 🖋 **Look at 1 and write.**

Sofia

After school, I **❶** _____ a jigsaw puzzle or I **❷** _____ the internet. On the weekend, I **❸** _____ for a walk or I **❹** _____ table tennis.

Hassan

In the afternoon, I **❺** _____ judo or I **❻** _____ a nap. On the weekend, I **❼** _____ a picnic or I **❽** _____ .

I can name free-time activities.

⏱ **Extra time?**

What other activities do you do? Write, draw, or say.

1 **Listen and check (✔).**

1 ⓐ  ⓑ  **2** ⓐ  ⓑ

 🧩 **Number and write.**

 listening

 They

to

aren't

music.

_____

2 🖊️ 💬 **Look and write. Draw two more friends and write about them. Then ask and answer.**

1 They aren't _____ .
They're _____ .
2 They're _____ .
They aren't _____ .

Are they bowling?

No, they aren't.

🕐 **Extra time?**

It's the weekend. What are your friends doing?

I can ask and answer about what people are doing.

The jigsaw puzzle

1 Read and write **Yes** or **No**.

❶ Amelia and Oscar are surfing the internet. _____

❷ In the jigsaw puzzle, two children are collecting shells. _____

❸ Oscar likes the jigsaw puzzle. _____

❹ Oscar and Amelia finish the jigsaw puzzle together. _____

2 Read and number in order.

ⓐ Amelia is sorry. ☐   ⓒ Oscar is mean. ☐

ⓑ Amelia is angry. ☐   ⓓ Oscar is sad. ☐

3 Do you like the story? Why? Circle.

I **like** / **don't like** this story because …

Amelia is nice.   Amelia is mean.   it's funny.   I like jigsaw puzzles.

the ending is happy.   Oscar is sad.

I can read and understand a story.

Extra time?
Tell your friend about
your favorite puzzle.

1 🖊 **Listen and number.**

Sing-along

2 🖊 🎵 SB 8.11 **Read, choose, and write. Then listen and check.**

| hide and seek |
| kick |
| play tag |
| slide   swing |

Do you want to play in the playground with me?

We can **1** _____ a ball.

We can **2** _____ and we can **3** _____ .

Do you want to play
in the playground with me?

🎵 Close your eyes.

Let's play **4** _____ .

Do you want to play
in the playground today?

🎵 We can **5** _____ .

Quick! Run away!

3 🖊 **Circle. What can you do in the playground?**

swing   play tag   do a jigsaw puzzle   collect shells

climb   slide   do homework   play hide and seek

 English at home

Sing the song for
your family!

I can name playground activities.

1 Read and circle.

He **is** / **isn't** taking a nap.

He **is** / **isn't** playing the guitar.

He **is** / **isn't** having a picnic.

He **is** / **isn't** helping.

Number and write.

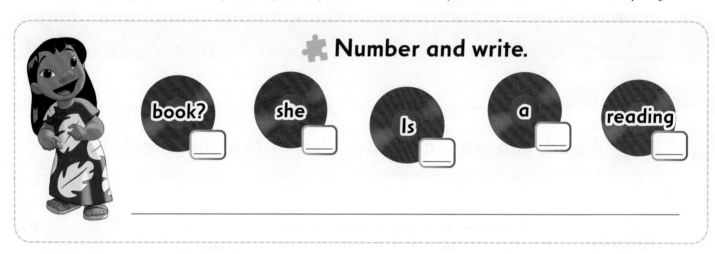

book?   she   Is   a   reading

_____

2 What's your friend doing? Choose and color two lines. Then write.

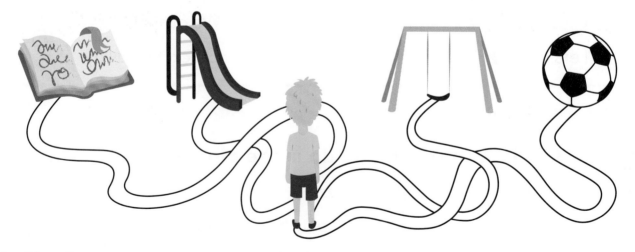

My friend's _____ .

My friend isn't _____ .

_____

I can ask and answer about what people are doing.

Extra time?

Guess your friend's sentences.

Noticing effects of behavior

1 🖉 **Look, read, and match.**

That's mean!

Thank you. That's nice.

I'm sorry! I feel bad.

Jack   Ellie   Katie   Oliver   Zoe   Luke

1 Jack is mean.

2 Katie is nice.

3 Luke is angry.

a Zoe is sorry.

b Ellie is angry.

c Oliver is happy.

2 💡 🖉 **What are the effects of your actions? Think and write.**

I'm nice. I help my brother with homework. My brother feels happy.

My portfolio

My actions	Effects
I'm ___nice___ . I _____ .	_____
I'm _____ . _____	_____

⭐**Be a hero!**⭐

Make a class kindness jar.

I can notice how my behavior affects others.

How things fly

1 🖊 **Trace. Then read and write Yes or No.**

1. Birds have engines. _____

2. A bird uses muscles to move its wings. _____

3. Planes move their wings up and down. _____

4. A plane has engines next to the wings. _____

5. Air pressure lifts the plane up. _____

2 🖊 **Look. Then write sentences with _too_.**

I can write

Birds have wings. Planes have wings, _too_.

1. Birds can fly. Planes can fly.

_____

2. Planes have engines. Cars have engines.

_____

3 💡 🖊 **What else can fly? Think of two more things or animals. Then write and draw.**

A _____ can fly.

_____

_____

I can understand and write about how things fly.

⏱ **Extra time?**

Show and tell a friend about your picture.

My free time poster

1 (Create) **Check (✔) and complete for your poster. Then write and draw.**

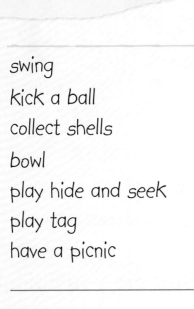

Our day out

	Me	My friend
swing	✔	
kick a ball		
collect shells		✔
bowl		
play hide and seek		
play tag		
have a picnic		
_____		
_____		

I'm swinging. My friend's collecting shells. We aren't kicking a ball.

Practice your presentation.

2 **How do you like to practice your presentation? Check (✔). Then practice.**

3 (Reflect) **Think and color.**

My project is ☆☆☆

 make and present a poster about my free-time activities.

⏱ **Extra time?**

Which project do you like best? Why?

My progress journal

1 🖊 **Find and circle five differences. Then read and write *a* or *b*.**

 ⓐ

 ⓑ

1 Daisy's swinging. ☐

3 Niko and Pedro are
playing hide and seek. ☐

5 Luiza's listening to music. ☐

2 Luiza's taking a nap. ☐

4 Amelia and Will are
kicking a ball. ☐

6 Laura's buying ice cream. ☐

2 🖊 **Choose and write. It's Saturday. What are you doing?
What are your friends doing?**

I _____ .

My friend _____

_____ .

My friends _____

_____ .

3 💡 🖊 **Think and draw ☹, ☺, or 😃.**

○   ○   ○   ○

**My favorite new
phrase is**

_____ .

Listening

1  **Listen and write.**

❶ What's the girl's name? _____Anna_____

❷ How many shells does she have? _____

❸ Who is taking a nap? _____

❹ What's the name of the little boy? _____

❺ How many ice cream cones is her mom buying? _____

Reading

2 **Read and write.**

tag   lemonade   shell   music

nap   swing   playground   picnic

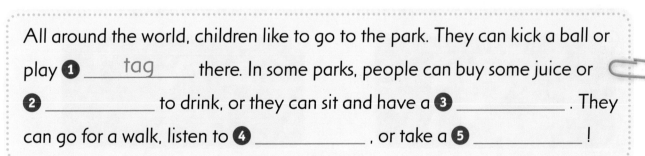

All around the world, children like to go to the park. They can kick a ball or play ❶ _____tag_____ there. In some parks, people can buy some juice or ❷ _____ to drink, or they can sit and have a ❸ _____ . They can go for a walk, listen to ❹ _____ , or take a ❺ _____ !

Speaking

3 **Look, point, and say. What's your favorite activity at the park? Draw it in 2.**

 Choose your favorite activity in the unit and stick.

9 Party time

Words I know	Words I want to learn
decorations banner balloons	_____
_____	_____
_____	_____

Video quiz

1 ▶ **9A** **Watch again and do the quiz.**

1 🖊 Read and circle.

Elsa's preparing a **party** / **picnic**.

Kristoff is **dancing** / **painting** the banner.

Olaf is **baking** / **eating** the cake.

Anna is in the **bedroom** / **kitchen**.

2 🖊 Read and circle.

One / **Two** / **Three** friends are helping Elsa.

2 🖉 **Choose and write.**

> balloons   banner   birthday cake
> decorations

1 _____

2 _____

3 _____

4 _____

3 Challenge! 🖉 **Find and write. What animal is Sven?**

1 n
2 d
3 r
4 i
5 e

Sven is a ___ ___ ___ ___ ___ ___ ___ ___ .
       3 5 4 1 2 5 5 3

🕐 **Extra time?**

Close your books.
Use the new words in
sentences.

I can name party things.

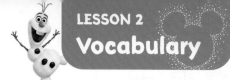

1 🖉 **Match. Then look and write the numbers.**

1 make   **2** blow out   **3** put up   **4** give

5 blow up   **6** decorate   **7** make goody   **8** invite

balloons   decorations   a gift   candles

a card   a cake   friends   bags

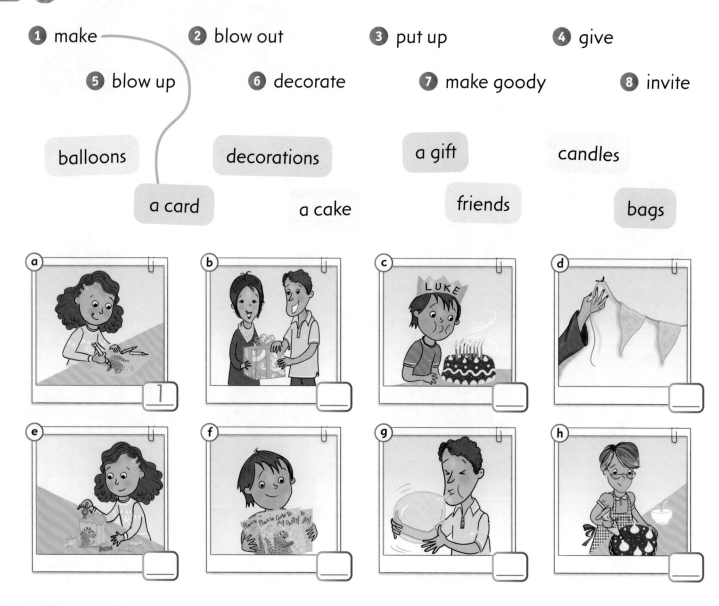

2 🖉 **Look at 1 and write. What are Luke and his family doing?**

1 His sister's making _____a card_____ and ___goody bags___ .

2 His parents are giving him _____ .

3 Luke is inviting _____ and blowing out _____ .

4 His mom's putting up _____ .

5 His dad's blowing up _____ .

6 His grandma's decorating _____ .

> ⏱ **Extra time?**
>
> What else can you do for a party? Write, draw, or say.

I can talk about party preparations.

1  **Listen and number.**

 a

 b

 c

 d

✲ **Number and write.**

are

doing?

What

they

_____

2 🖊 💬 **Look, complete, and match. Then ask and answer.**

blow   decorate   make (x2)   ~~put~~

Layla   Tara   Connor   Ollie   Rosa

Simon   Harry

1 Harry's

2 Layla's

3 Simon's

4 Rosa and Ollie are

5 Tara and Connor are

ⓐ _____ a banner.

ⓑ _____ a cake.

ⓒ _putting_ up decorations.

ⓓ _____ a card.

ⓔ _____ up balloons.

What's Harry doing?

⏱ **Extra time?**

Draw you in 2. What are you doing? Write or tell a friend.

I can ask and answer about what people are doing.

103

The party

1 🖊 **Look, read, and match.**

ⓐ Dad's in charge.

ⓑ Wow! Thank you.

ⓒ I'm decorating the cake.

ⓓ Let's work together.

2 🖊 **Check (✔). Who helps to get ready for the party? Then count and write the number.**

_____ people help to get ready.

3 💡 🖊 **Do you like the story? Color.**

I don't like it.   It's OK.   I like it.   I like it a lot.   I love it!

I can read and understand a story.

🕐 **Extra time?**

Imagine you are Luiza. How do you feel?

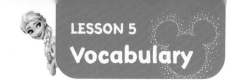

1 ✏️ **Read, choose, and write.**   Claudia   David   Rafa   Sally

1 _____
2 _____
3 _____
4 _____
5 _____

Claudia's eating popcorn. She's wearing a party hat.

Rafa isn't wearing a party hat. He's eating watermelon and drinking lemonade.

David's eating watermelon too. He's wearing a party hat.

Sally isn't wearing a hat. She's wearing a mask.

2 ✏️ **Look at 1 and find Marcus. Choose and write.**

candy   lemonade   mask   party hat   popcorn   watermelon

1 Marcus is wearing a _____ .
2 He isn't wearing a _____ .

3 He's eating _____ .
4 He's drinking _____ .

5 He isn't eating _____ or _____ .

3 ✏️ **Think about party things and write.**

What can you wear?	What can you eat or drink?
mask	cake
____ ____	____ ____
____ ____	____ ____

🏠 **English at home**

Sing the song for your family!

I can name party things.

105

1 ✏️ **Look, read, and match.**

1. It's Elsa's   ⓐ boots.
2. They're Kristoff's   ⓑ shoes.
3. They're Anna's   ⓒ dress.

🧩 **Number and write.**

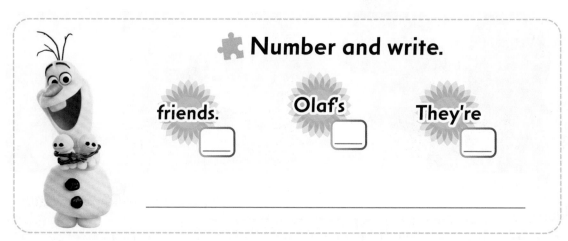

friends. ☐   Olaf's ☐   They're ☐

_____

2 ✏️ 💬 **Join the dots and write. Then ask and answer.**

It's ____Kim's cake____ .

They're _____ .

balloons ~~cake~~
flowers party hat

It's _____ .

They're _____ .

What's this?

It's Ren's party hat.

🕐 **Extra time?**

Find and draw something that isn't yours. Whose is it? Write or say.

I can ask and answer about who things belong to.

LESSON 7
Myself and others
Responsible decision-making

Sharing tasks

1 ✏️ 🎧 **Look and circle. Who's helping? Then listen, choose, and write.**

9.2

| get ready | in charge |
| prepare | |

1 Let's _____ for spring.

2 Miss Jess is _____.

3 First, let's _____ the soil.

2 💡 ✏️ **Plan a goodbye party for your class.**

Goodbye party plan

day: _____

time: _____

food and drinks: _____

_____

decorations: _____

_____

My portfolio

Who can help? What can they do?

name	task

⭐**Be a hero!**⭐
Make posters for your party.

I can share tasks in a team.

107

Rosemaling patterns

1 Read and check (✔).

1 Which picture shows a pattern?

 a    b

2 Which picture shows symmetry?

 a    b

3 Which pattern uses a paintbrush?

 a    b

4 Which pattern has curvy lines?

 a    b

2 ✏️ Look. Then circle the describing words.

 **I can write**

You can put (blue) and (white) paint on the paintbrush.
1 There are curvy lines in my picture.
2 I have blue, green, and purple crayons.

3 💡 ✏️ Design a pattern and write. Use describing words.

My pattern is a _____ .
It has _____ lines.
I use _____ and
_____ paint.

⏱ Extra time?

Show and tell a friend about your pattern.

I can understand and write about patterns.

My cake design

1 Think about your cake design. Read and check (✔).

I know what to do. ◯

My materials are
on my desk. ◯

I know what information
I need. ◯

I know how to ask
for help. ◯

I want to do
good work. ◯

I'm ready to work. ◯

Check you have the
things you need.

Check you have the
information you need.

Do your best.

2 (Create) Think and complete for your cake.
Then write and draw.

Who is it for? _____

How old is **she** / **he**? _____

She / **He** likes **the ocean** / **animals** /
sport / **flowers** / _____

What is **her** / **his** favorite color? _____

My cake is for Alejandro. He's eight.
His favorite color is orange.

My cake

_____

_____

3 (Reflect) Think and color.

My project is ☆☆☆

⏱ Extra time?

Tell your friend about
your cake design.

My progress journal

1 🖊️ **Look, read, and write Yes or No.**

a

1 It's a grocery store. _____

2 There are six masks. _____

3 Two people are wearing party hats. _____

4 There are eight candles on the cake. _____

5 Pedro's backpack is yellow. _____

6 Amelia's party hat is pink. _____

2 🖊️ **Look at 1 and answer.**

| blow up   buy   eat   make   put up |

1 What's Amelia doing? _____

2 What are Pedro and Niko doing? _____

3 What are Sarah and Mary doing? _____

4 What's Neil doing? _____

5 What's Linda doing? _____

3 💡 🖊️ **Think and draw** ☹️, 🙂, **or** 😄**.**

My favorite party word is

_____.

Listening

1 Listen and write.

1 What's the girl's name? _____Alice_____

2 How old is she? _____

3 What's the boy's name? _____

4 Where does he live? _____ Street

5 How many balloons are there? _____

Reading

2 Look, read, and write.

1 Where are they?

They're in the ___kitchen___ .

2 What's the girl doing?

She's _____ balloons.

3 What's the boy making?

He's making a _____ .

4 What color is Mom's mask?

It's _____ .

5 How many gifts are there?

There are _____ gifts.

6 What are the children wearing on their heads?

They're wearing _____ .

Speaking

3 Answer the questions for you.

How old are you?

Do you like lemonade?   Can you bake a cake?   What are you wearing?

 Choose your favorite activity in the unit and stick.

Pearson Education Limited
KAO Two
KAO Park
Hockham Way
Harlow, Essex
CM17 9SR
England
and Associated Companies throughout the world.

pearsonenglish.com
© Pearson Education Limited 2022

First published 2022
ISBN: 978-1-292-44164-1
Set in Arta Medium 19/25pt

Printed in Slovakia by Neografia

Image Credits:
123RF.com: Ferli 46, Gresei 43, Igor Korionov 72, Liliia Rudchenko 108, Mariia Voloshina 43, Muksab 108, NORIKAZU SATOMI 43, Photochicken 84, PV productions 84, Thidarat Suriyawong 43, Yaroslav Olieinikov 85, Yurakp 43; **Getty Images:** Ian.CuiYi/Moment 108, Jeremy Walker/Stone 108, Nina Erhart / EyeEm 66, Patrick Lane/Corbis 85, Todd Warnock/ Digital Vision 9, Tuan Tran/ Stone 43; **Shutterstock:** Aliaksandra Spirydovich 43, Amelia Martin 60, Andy Dean Photography 66, BEST-BACKGROUNDS 72, Cavan Images - Offset 9, Chatchawal Kittirojana 84, Colin Porteous 96, Dani Vincek 43, DeawSS 60, EDHAR 84, Kurt 108, Lemusique 95, Lifestyle Graphic 11, 23, 35, 47, 59, 71, 83, 95, 107, Marekuliasz 108, Markus Gann 72, MBI 85, MONOPOLY919 84, Nalinda117 66, Nick Vorobey 96, Photka 13, 14, 23, 26, 35, 37, 38, 47, 50, 59, 61, 71, 74, 85, 86, 95, 97, 99, 109, 110, SARAWUT KUNDEJ 24, Sofy 66, ZouZou 43.

Illustrations
Alan Brown/Advocate Art p. 59 (activity 2); **Begoña Fernández Corbalan/ Advocate Art** pp. 6, 11 (activity 1), 19, 21 (activity 1), 22 (activity 2), 27 (activity 2), 47 (activity 1), 49, 51, 54, 55, 63 (activity 1), 66, 70, 73, 75 (activity 2), 87 (activity 1), 91, 95, 99 (activity 1), 103; **Samara Hardy with help from Jana Curl/Plum Pudding** (course characters); **Jen Jamieson/Plum Pudding** pp. 9, 15 (activity 1), 23, 59 (activity 1), 71, 93, 99 (activity 2), 105, 107; **Jo Parry/Advocate Art** pp. 62 (activity 1), 63 (activity 2); **Adriana Puglisi/Plum Pudding** pp. 15 (activity 2), 21 (activity 2), 22 (activity 1), 42, 57, 58, 61, 79, 102, 106, 111; **Sean Simms/Advocate Art** pp. 11 (activity 2), 12, 30 (spots), 39 (spots), 47 (activity 2), 67, 69, 74 (clocks), 75 (activity 2), 85, 98; **Diego Vaisberg/Advocate Art** pp. 2, 30 (scene), 31, 33, 34, 36, 39 (scene), 83, 90, 94; **Steven Wood/Advocate Art** pp. 18, 25, 27 (activity 2), 35, 45, 46, 78, 81, 87 (activity 2), 97; **Evelt Yanait/Advocate Art** pp. 43.